Test Your Vocabulary – Book 2

Peter Watcyn-Jones

Illustrated by Sven Nordqvist

PENGUIN
ENGLISH

PENGUIN ENGLISH

Published by the Penguin Group
Penguin Books Ltd, 27 Wrights Lane, London W8 5TZ, England
Penguin Books USA Inc., 375 Hudson Street, New York, New York 10014, USA
Penguin Books Australia Ltd, Ringwood, Victoria, Australia
Penguin Books Canada Ltd, 10 Alcorn Avenue, Toronto, Ontario, Canada M4V 3B2
Penguin Books (NZ) Ltd, 182-190 Wairau Road, Auckland 10, New Zealand

Penguin Books Ltd, Registered Offices: Harmondsworth, Middlesex, England

First published in Sweden by Kursverksamhetens förlag 1979
Published in Penguin Books 1985
20 19 18 17 16 15 14 13

Printed and bound in Great Britain by
BPC Hazell Books Ltd
A member of
The British Printing Company Ltd
Set in Times

CONTENTS

INTRODUCTION

Owing to the emphasis in recent years on functional and communicative approaches to language learning, many other important areas of the language have been neglected. One such area is vocabulary. This series is an attempt to remedy this situation not only by filling a real gap in the materials available but also by attempting to show that vocabulary learning can be just as much fun and just as stimulating as other activities. There are five books altogether in the series, ranging from Elementary level to Advanced. Each book contains fifty tests or exercises and, to facilitate self-study, a key is also included. Students using these books should find vocabulary learning both stimulating and enjoyable and, hopefully, start to develop a real sensitivity to the language.

Test Your Vocabulary – Book 2 is the third book in the series and is intended for intermediate students. There are approximately 800 words in the book and the tests closely follow those in *Test Your Vocabulary – Book 1* both in layout and in areas of vocabulary, for example, things in the home, jobs, clothes, people's characteristics, and so on. Again, there are twelve picture tests which concentrate on everyday objects in the home, furniture, parts of the car, etc. Finally, there are tests based on words and prepositions which pose particular problems for foreign learners.

TO THE STUDENT

This book will help you to learn a lot of new English words. But in order for the new words to become "fixed" in your mind, you need to test yourself again and again. Here is one method you can use to help you learn the words:

1. Read through the instructions carefully for the test you are going to try. Then try the test, writing your answers **in pencil**.
2. When you have finished, check your answers and correct any mistakes you have made. Read through the test again, paying special attention to the words you didn't know or got wrong.
3. Try the test again five minutes later. You can do this either by covering up the words (for example, in the picture tests) or by asking a friend to test you. Repeat this until you can remember all the words.
4. **Rub out your answers**.
5. Try the test again the following day. (You should remember most of the words.)
6. Finally, plan to try the test at least twice again within the following month. After this most of the words will be "fixed" in your mind.

1 Things in the home 1

Write the number of each drawing next to the correct word.

coat hanger	12
potato peeler	.....
lightbulb	.....
colander	.....
broom	.....
plate	.....
egg slicer	.....
dustpan	.....
carpet beater	.....
scrubbing brush	.....
cheese slicer	.....
tea towel	.....

1

2 Synonyms – adjectives

Give a synonym for each of the words in brackets in the following sentences. Choose from the ones below. Number 1 has been done for you.

odd	bashful	attractive	authentic
cheeky	enjoyable	unbelievable	obstinate
enormous	ample	big-headed	appalling
hilarious	vital	keen	

1 He was one of the most (good-looking) *attractive* men she had ever seen.

2 We had a really (pleasant) .... time in Brighton last week.

3 David is always telling people how good he is at everything. He's so (conceited) ....

4 The play last night was (terrible) .... At least half the audience walked out in the middle of it.

5 There's something very (peculiar) .... about Mr Brown's behaviour today. Haven't you noticed?

6 Have you seen James and Sally's new house? It's really (huge) ....

7 He won't take my advice. He's so (stubborn) ....

8 I was always very (shy) .... as a child and hated going to parties or meeting new people.

9 My son loves school. In fact, in some ways he's too (enthusiastic) .... I mean, it's the only thing he ever talks about.

10 It looked like (a genuine) an .... Picasso, but in fact it was only a copy.

11 I think Martha is going to have a lot of problems with her children. They're so (rude) .... to everyone.

12 You should have done it by now. You've had (sufficient) .... time.

13 You must read this story – it's quite (incredible) .... !

14 Hard work and ambition are (essential) .... if you want to get on in life.

15 You must go and see the new "Monty Python" film – it's (very funny) ....

3 Where do they live?

Read through the following sentences and fill in the missing words.

1 Most English families live in a . . . . .
2 A king lives in a . . . .
3 A monk lives in a . . . .
4 A nun lives in a . . . .
5 Soldiers live in a . . . .
6 A prisoner lives in a . . . .
7 A gipsy lives in a . . . .
8 An eskimo lives in an . . . .
9 A bee lives in a . . . .
10 A bird lives in a . . . .
11 A dog lives in a . . . .
12 A horse lives in a . . . .
13 A pig lives in a . . . .
14 A spider lives in a . . . .
15 An eagle lives in an . . . .

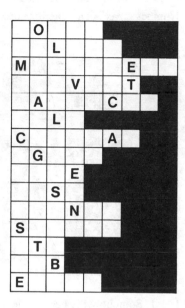

4 A true story

Look at the following cartoon-strip of something that really happened. Then try to work out which sentence goes with which drawing. Number the sentences 1–10. Number 1 has been done for you.

A TRUE STORY

(   )   Somehow the bees made a hole in the paper and climbed up the man's legs.

(   )   Officials noticed a man without trousers and thought he was an escaped lunatic.

(   )   To avoid being stung by the bees, he explained his dilemma to the women in the compartment, who left.

(   )   They wrapped round the neck of a ticket inspector, who was attacked by the bees.

(1)   A few years ago, a Hungarian was travelling by train to Budapest.

(   )   It took the bee expert three days to convince doctors at the Mental Hospital that he was sane.

(   )   He took off his trousers – and an express train travelling in the opposite direction set up such a draught that his trousers flew out into the corridor.

(   )   He was arrested and put in a strait-jacket.

(   )   He had some bees in a milk bottle which was covered with brown paper.

(   )   Someone pulled the communication cord, the train pulled up and caught fire.

5 Things in the home 2

Write the number of each drawing next to the correct word.

pepper mill	. . . . .
liquidizer/blender	. . . . .
fire guard	. . . . .
bowl	. . . . .
tray	. . . . .
briefcase	. . . . .
lemon squeezer	. . . . .
tea strainer	. . . . .
bellows	. . . . .
bottle opener	. . . . .
suitcase	. . . . .
ladle	. . . . .

6 Opposites – adjectives

Find the opposites of the words on the left. Choose from the ones on the right.
Number 1 has been done for you.

ADJECTIVE	OPPOSITE
1 harmless	*harmful*
2 generous	
3 permanent	
4 industrious	
5 gigantic	
6 friendly	
7 dull	
8 daring	
9 dear	
10 narrow-minded	
11 real	
12 horrible	
13 gradual	
14 keen	
15 fortunate	

lazy
broad-minded
timid
sudden
unfortunate
mean
wonderful
hostile
temporary
uninterested
exciting
cheap
imaginary
harmful
minute

7 Countries and nationalities

Fill in the following crossword and see how many countries and nationalities you can remember.

DOWN

1 This person has no trouble buying petrol.
2 The river Ganges flows through this country.
3 This person lives in a country near France, where they speak two languages.
4 This person lives in a country whose capital is Prague.
5 They play a lot of ice-hockey in this country.
6 .... people make very good bankers.
7 A native of Poland.
8 A very famous ....is Victor Borge.
9 Both Iraq and Iran border this country.
10 These people live in south-east Asia.
11 A country with a famous canal.
12 See above ....

ACROSS

1 A native of one of the countries of Scandinavia.
2 A small country whose capital is Wellington.
3 They grow tulips in this country.
4 One of the countries of Gt. Britain.
5 Both an island and a continent.
6 The bazouki is a typical ....instrument.
7 This person suffered a lot under Hitler.
8 A country in South America.
9 A country full of fjords.
10 This person loves cold weather.
11 Large country in North America.

8 Quantities

Fill in the correct phrase under each drawing.

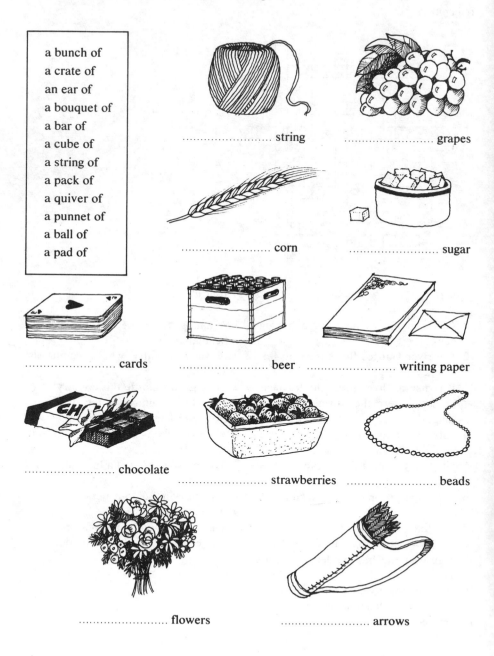

a bunch of
a crate of
an ear of
a bouquet of
a bar of
a cube of
a string of
a pack of
a quiver of
a punnet of
a ball of
a pad of

.... string

.... grapes

.... corn

.... sugar

.... cards

.... beer

.... writing paper

.... chocolate

.... strawberries

.... beads

.... flowers

.... arrows

9 Things in the home 3

Write the number of each drawing next to the correct word.

chopping board	....
aerial	....
banister	....
curtains	....
door handle	....
doorbell	....
coffee filter	....
pillow	....
dustbin	....
umbrella	....
spatula	....
cushion	....

10 Choose the word 1

Choose the word which best completes each sentence.

1 A bed on board a ship is called a ....
   a sleeper   b cabin   c bunk   d dormitory

2 I have no brothers or sisters. I am .... child.
   a an only   b a sole   c a unique   d a single

3 I'm terribly sorry, I seem to have .... my book at home.
   a lost   b forgotten   c left   d hidden

4 My sister and I are always quarrelling. We just don't seem to ....
   a get off   b get together   c get on   d get by

5 Most parents find it difficult to .... their children nowadays.
   a grow up   b foster   c develop   d bring up

6 I .... to inform you that your mother died ten minutes ago.
   a sorry   b regret   c apologise   d pity

7 I think everyone should .... the Human Rights movement.
   a agree   b support   c stand up   d supply

8 I only paid £3 for this dress. It was a real ....
   a find   b sale   c bargain   d cheap

9 I always try to .... something each month for my holidays.
   a save   b spare   c spend   d put

10 I don't have a job. I'm ....
   a lonely   b sick   c unused   d unemployed

11 Which horse shall we .... on in the 2.15 race?
   a back   b bet   c place   d win

12 Manchester United .... Liverpool in the F.A. Cup Final.
   a beat   b won   c sailed   d lost

11 Guess their jobs

Read through the following sentences and then write down which job each of the following people have.

1. MISS REES 2. MR BERRY 3. MR. GUARD 4. MRS. KNOWLES 5. MR TRAIN
6. MRS PLOD 7. MRS CARTER 8. MR AUSTIN 9. MR FIELD 10. MISS SAYER

1 You go to this person when you want to take out some money at a bank.
2 This person helps you when you play golf by carrying your clubs and giving you advice.
3. This person looks after a block of flats or an office.
4. When you have a legal problem, you can always go to this person.
5. He carries your bags for you at the station.
6. This person delivers letters.
7 This person performs operations at a hospital.
8 If you have a lot of money, you might employ this person to drive you around.
9 This person keeps animals and grows crops.
10 If you have a problem with your speech, this person can help you overcome it.

Miss Rees is a c ....   Mrs Plod is a p ....
Mr Berry is a c ....   Mrs Carter is a s ....
Mr Guard is a c.....................   Mr Austin is a c ....
Miss Knowles is a s ....   Mr Field is a f ....
Mr Train is a p ....   Miss Sayer is a s .... t ....

12   The name of the room

Read through the sentences and fill in the missing words.

1 A room in a hospital where people needing treatment stay.

2 A room in a house or flat where you usually do the cooking.

3 A room under a house.

4 A room at the top of a house, under the roof. It is often used for storing things.

5 Small rooms on board a ship where the crew and passengers sleep.

6 A room used for studying or working.

7 A room under a church.

8 The part of a ship below deck where goods are stored.

9 A room in a house where food is stored.

10 A room in a house used by a family for receiving guests – a sort of "best room".
(It is not so common nowadays.)

11 A room where an artist or photographer works.

12 A large, comfortable room for sitting, found at a hotel.

13 A room with lots of beds used for sleeping, e.g. at a boarding school.

13 Tools, etc.

Write the number of each drawing next to the correct word.

plane	. . . . .
file	. . . . .
axe	. . . . .
pliers	. . . . .
extension cable	. . . . .
jack	. . . . .
secateurs	. . . . .
watering can	. . . . .
sickle	. . . . .
vice	. . . . .
fire extinguisher	. . . . .
chisel	. . . . .

14 Synonyms – verbs

Give a synonym for each of the words in brackets in the following sentences. Choose from the ones below. (Make any other necessary changes.) Number 1 has been done for you.

detest	purchase	spoil	trip
inform	accomplish	put off	alter
enter	moan	recollect	occur
brag	vanish	scare	

1 Being a gentleman, I allowed the women to (go in) ....*enter*.......... first.

2 They were all watching the U.F.O. when it suddenly (disappeared) ....

3 This is something I (bought) .... from an antique dealer in Chelsea.

4 I love watching football, but my wife (loathes) .... it.

5 He (stumbled) .... and fell as he was leaving the church.

6 You won't (achieve) .... anything if you don't work harder.

7 The manuscript is basically good – but there are still parts of it that need to be (changed) ....

8 I couldn't (remember) .... where I had first met her.

9 The match has been (postponed) .... until next week.

10 Alfred Hitchcock's films really (frighten) .... me; especially the one he made about a lot of birds attacking people.

11 Bad weather completely (ruined) .... the Garden Party.

12 I don't like the new secretary very much – she's always (complaining) .... about something or other.

13 Can you tell me in your own words exactly what (happened) ....?

14 Would you please (notify) .... me the moment Miss Baker gets back?

15 I can't stand Doreen. She's always (boasting) .... about the places she's been to.

14

15 Find the buildings

On the following map are ten buildings. Read through the information below and then write down the names of the various buildings.

Building number 1 is always full on Sundays.

The Local Council meet once a week at the building in Kenilworth Road.

The building near the railway bridge is full of old things, including the skeleton of a dinosaur.

Building number 8 is very high.

Building number 10 is surrounded by walls 20 feet high.

If you are looking for a house or a flat you should go to Croft Road.

When driving from Coventry, take the second turning on the right to get to St. Mary's.

There's a Van Gogh Exhibition on this week in Beswick Road.

They're showing "Star Wars" at the building at the corner of Newcombe Road and Station Road.

When my father died we ordered a coffin from the building in London Road South. The building at the corner of Croft Road and Knowles Avenue is divided into offices. Building number 5 is where you can go to put a bet on a horse.

Building number 1 is a ....

Building number 2 is an .... (2 words)

Building number 3 is a ....

Building number 4 is an .... (2 words)

Building number 5 is a .... (2 words)

Building number 6 is a ....

Building number 7 is an ....

Building number 8 is an .... (2 words)

Building number 9 is the .... (2 words)

Building number 10 is a ....

16 Word association 1

Each of the following groups of four words is in some way connected with the same thing. Write down this word for each of the groups. Number 1 has been done for you.

1 clutch, motorway, drive, Volvo

2 referee, penalty, corner, Leeds

3 percussion, symphony, conductor, violins

4 petal, stem, rose, garden

5 collar, tail, bark, Alsatian

6 bride, ring, church, photographer

7 kitchen, stairs, family, address

8 string, Segovia, fret, chord

9 pillow, night, mattress, snore

10 telescope, Venus, galaxy, science

11 gun, war, fight, uniform

12 waveband, transistor, aerial, tuner

13 key, letter, secretary, ribbon

14 landlord, glass, darts, bar

15 umpire, net, set, court

16 eat, potatoes, lunch, cook

17 bank, Danube, flow, estuary

18 heel, lace, sole, wear

19 matron, ward, patient, illness

20 crotchet, compose, treble clef, classical

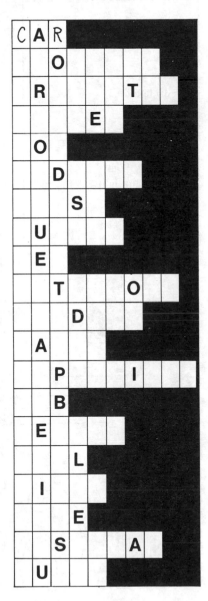

17 Furniture and fittings 1

Write the number of each drawing next to the correct word.

stove (cooker)	. . . . .
washing machine	. . . . .
fridge	. . . . .
coffee table	. . . . .
bedside table	. . . . .
shower	. . . . .
bath	. . . . .
wardrobe	. . . . .
broom cupboard	. . . . .
fluorescent light	. . . . .
oil lamp	. . . . .
ceiling light	. . . . .

18 Missing words – people's characteristics

Put the following words in the correct sentences.

ambitious	big-headed	intelligent	immature
rude	obstinate	moody	eccentric
strict	sympathetic		

1 John is always telling people how well he plays the guitar. He's so ....
....

2 Many girls of 16 and 17 are far too .... to get married and have children.

3 I see Clive's passed all his exams again. It must be wonderful to be so ....
....

4 The trouble with Jane is that she's so .... One minute she's laughing, the next she's sulking. You just don't know where you are with her.

5 One of the things I like about Pamela is that she's so ....
If you have a problem you know you can go to her and that she'll listen to you and try to help all she can.

6 Mrs Green's children are so .... They never say "Please" or "Thank you" and only last week I heard them swearing at the postman.

7 My son's very .... He doesn't want to work in an office all his life. In fact he keeps telling me that one day he's going to be Prime Minister.

8 My uncle is very .... No matter what the weather, he always wears a bright red cape when he goes out and a matching pair of boots. Everyone stares at him, but he doesn't mind. He likes being different.

9 My husband never sees my point of view. He has his opinions and nothing I say will ever change them. He's so ....

10 When I was a teenager, my father was very .... He'd never allow me to wear make-up or have a boyfriend, and if I went out with friends I always had to be home by 10 o'clock.

19 Hobbies and pastimes

Fill in the following crossword. Each answer is a hobby or pastime.

ACROSS

1 An outdoor activity for those who like running and map reading.
2 Not on land.
3 A useful activity which some people can do at the same time as watching TV.
4 An interest in the ancient world. May spend weekends digging somewhere.
5 A popular card game.
6 An activity which is never finished. Can't be done in a flat.
7 You need a loom to do this properly.
8 A good way to spend the weekend. But not as comfortable as a hotel!
9 A creative hobby. You may even sell one or two of the things you create.
10 An indoor game for 2–4 players. (2 words)
11 Most people are interested in this whether they play an instrument or not.
12 A relaxing activity. You may spend hours on your head!

DOWN

1 All you need is a camera.
2 A relaxing activity, mainly done by women. Could be called painting with wool, nylon, etc.
3 It's the closest thing to being a bird.
4 A hobby which can also be a good investment. (2 words)
5 A good way to keep fit and of getting around.
6 A popular board game. Often takes hours.
7 A popular hobby where the thing you make disappears once you make it.
8 If you do this then you'll know how to do the rumba, samba, etc.
9 You need an animal to do this.
10 A popular summer pastime – especially when the weather is warm.
11 A pastime for those who fancy themselves as Richard Burton and Elizabeth Taylor.
12 A winter pastime. Can be done indoors or out-of-doors. (2 words)
13 A famous Chinese game, played with tiles. (2 words)
14 An indoor game with balls.
15 A relaxing, outdoor hobby where you sit for hours before anything happens.
16 A creative hobby using clay.

20 Prepositions 1

Put in the missing prepositions in the following sentences.

1 I'm very disappointed .... him.

    a on   b in   c of

2 Who else was .... the party on Saturday?

    a at   b on   c to

3 He had difficulty .... starting the car.

    a with   b to   c in

4 What do English people eat .... Christmas?

    a to   b at   c under

5 That music was written .... Beethoven.

    a of   b with   c by

6 I'm very conscious .... my big nose.

    a of   b at   c with

7 The police car chased the robbers .... the streets.

    a among   b in   c through

8 I'm looking .... my lighter. Have you seen it?

    a to   b after   c for

9 I haven't smoked .... ages.

    a for   b since   c at

10 I'm tired .... learning English.

    a on   b of   c with

11 Here – divide this bar of chocolate .... yourselves.

    a in   b among   c with

12 His opinion differs .... mine.

    a to   b from   c with

13 You go on – there's no need to wait .... me.

    a on   b by   c for

14 If you don't know what a word means, you can always look it .... in a dictionary.

    a on   b over   c up

15 He was very proud .... being English.

    a of   b over   c with

21 Furniture and fittings 2

Write the number of each drawing next to the correct word.

shaving socket . . . . .
record storage unit . . . . .
time switch . . . . .
window sill . . . . .
fan heater . . . . .
trolley . . . . .
room divider . . . . .
door knob . . . . .
extractor fan . . . . .
curtain rail . . . . .
coat stand . . . . .
window box . . . . .

22 Puzzle it out 1 – Who's who in Susan's family?

Read through the sentences below, then see if you can work out the relationship between the various people and Susan.

BILL   TED   ANNE   FREDA   OLIVE   PAUL

Bill is Ted's father.
Freda is Olive's daughter.
Anne's husband has a beard.
Paul is Ted's brother-in-law.
Olive is Bill's sister.
Susan's father wears glasses.

Bill is Susan's   . . . .
Ted is Susan's   . . . .
Anne is Susan's   . . . .
Freda is Susan's   . . . .
Olive is Susan's   . . . .
Paul is Susan's   . . . .

23 Animal sounds

Fill in the correct verb under each drawing.

lows
barks
trumpets
croaks
neighs
bleats
roars
squeaks
grunts
crows

a pig ....

a dog ....

a mouse ....

a cock ....

a frog ....

an elephant ....

a horse ....

a lamb ....

a lion ....

a cow ....

24 Find the words

Fill in the missing first and last letters in the words below. A clue is given for each word.

#						Clue
1	H	R	O	A		part of the body
2	A	T	U	R		a planet
3	A	L	L	E		a container for money
4	A	B	B	I		an animal
5	A	U	C	E		a piece of crockery
6	P	I	D	E		an insect
7	I	L	L	O		a tree
8	A	L	M	O		a fish
9	A	N	I	S		to disappear
10	L	O	U	S		a piece of clothing
11	K	I	I	N		a sport
12	I	G	H	T		a number
13	I	G	E	O		a bird
14	A	W	Y	E		a job
15	U	I	T	A		a musical instrument
16	E	P	H	E		a relative
17	I	Z	A	R		a reptile
18	A	D	I	S		a vegetable
19	E	T	R	O		Americans call it gasoline
20	U	T	T	E		a pipe at the bottom of a roof to carry away rainwater

25 Newspaper misprints

In each of the following extracts from a newspaper there is a misprint. Write down the word which is wrong and also write down which word should have been used instead.

	Misprint	Correct word
1 He is now being kept alive by an artificial respirator and huge doses of rugs.	rugs	drugs
2 The route taken by the King and Queen was lined by clapping, cheering crows.		
3 Barry Jones was seriously burnt last weekend when he came in contact with a high voltage wife.		
4 Congratulations and best wishes to my daring fiancée on her 21st birthday.		
5 He was taken to hospital with heard injuries.		
6 Young lady required for publishing company. Previous experience not essential bust must be able to type.		
7 1969 Volvo. One owner. God. Low mileage.		
8 A neighbour also claims to have seen the ghost and it upset him so much that he has not eaten property for several days.		
9 The bank robbers tried to escape but were cornered by a polite dog.		
10 Heat a very small amount of oil in a frying pan. Fry meatballs, burning them as they cook for about 15 minutes.		

26 Clothes

Write the number of each drawing next to the correct word.

bow tie	. . . . .
bowler hat	. . . . .
beret	. . . . .
cardigan	. . . . .
sweater	. . . . .
apron	. . . . .
gloves	. . . . .
braces	. . . . .
clogs	. . . . .
shorts	. . . . .
sandals	. . . . .
string vest	. . . . .

27 Choose the word 2

Choose the word which best completes each sentence.

1 My work's got worse and worse. Unless I .... I'll fail my exams in the summer.

  a get well   b improve   c increase   d get back

2 Oh dear! My watch has ....!

  a ended   b stopped   c finished   d completed

3 If you work for someone, then you are ....

  a a slave   b unemployed   c an employer   d an employee

4 I'm afraid there's no .... of seeing Mr Brown until tomorrow.

  a possibility   b wish   c opportunity   d chance

5 The .... around this town is quite beautiful.

  a countryside   b scene   c nature   d country

6 He's always telling me what to do. He's so ....

  a cruel   b bossy   c helpful   d charming

7 His parents gave him everything he asked for. He was thoroughly ....

  a disturbed   b ashamed   c full up   d spoilt

8 I still feel like a cigarette even though I .... smoking two years ago.

  a gave in   b gave up   c gave over   d completed

9 He wants to get to the top before he is thirty. He is very ....

  a tall   b ambitious   c intelligent   d industrial

10 John always arrives on time. He's so ....

  a careful   b boring   c punctual   d timeless

11 She made the .... mistake of forgetting to put the "s" on the verb in the third person singular.

  a classic   b important   c classical   d famous

12 I was very .... for all the advice she gave me.

  a glad   b grateful   c in debt   d pleased

28 Phrases

Fill in the missing words in the following drawings. Choose an appropriate phrase from the ones below:

a Yes, I think so.

b Yes, that would be nice.

c Yes, very funny.

d Not at all.

e No, I don't think I have.

f Yes – do help yourself.

g How about going to the pictures?

h No, there's no need, thanks.

i No, not just now, thanks.

j It was great fun.

k No, not very.

l That's rubbish!

29 Complete the dialogue

In the following dialogue, the part of Paul has been left out. Put in the words he speaks in the right order from the phrases below.

- About a month ago.
- St. Richard's Comprehensive?
- Well, as a matter of fact, we've decided to get a divorce.
- Oh, sorry!
- (Laughing) I see. Still the same old John. You haven't changed a bit!
- Yes, that's right. Sweden.
- You must enjoy it there, then.
- Oh, I live here now.
- No, only me.
- Ah well, it can't be helped. And there aren't any children fortunately.
- John! This is a surprise!
- But anyway, enough of me. What are you doing these days?

Paul: ....

John: That's all right.

Paul: ....

John: Paul! Paul Jennings! Well I never! What on earth are you doing here?

Paul: ....

John: Do you? But the last I heard of you, you were teaching abroad somewhere.

Paul: ....

John: So when did you come back?

Paul: ....

John: And is Sally with you?

Paul: ....

John: Only you?

Paul: ....

John: Oh, I am sorry to hear that, Paul.

Paul: ....

John: Yes, that's one blessing, I suppose.

Paul: ....

John: Oh, still teaching, you know. Same school as before.

Paul: ....

John: That's the one.

Paul: ....

John: Well, let's just say it helps pay the rent, shall we?

Paul: ....

John: No, neither have you. I'd have recognised you anywhere.

30 Sports, games, pastimes – equipment

Write the number of each drawing next to the correct word or words.

dartboard	.....
tennis racquet	.....
badminton racquet	.....
air pistol	.....
golf club	.....
tent	.....
chess set	.....
dice	.....
figure skate	.....
ski stick	.....
shin pad	.....
dumbbell	.....
shuttlecock	.....
binoculars	.....
ice hockey stick	.....

31 Where do you find them?

Here are 40 words arranged in alphabetical order. Work out where you are most likely to find them and write them down under the appropriate words. (There are five words under each.)

aisle, altar, blackboard, boot, bumper, button, clutch, collar, congregation, crew, cutlery, date stamp, deck, desks, dishwasher, filing cabinet, fridge, frying pan, funnel, horn, lapel, matron, operating theatre, patients, pew, playground, pocket, portholes, pulpit, pupils, rails, seatbelt, secretary, sink unit, sleeve, staffroom, stapler, stethoscope, typewriter, ward.

1 in a school

....
....
....
....
....

2 in the kitchen

....
....
....
....
....

3 on a boat

....
....
....
....
....

4 in a church

....
....
....
....
....

5 on a jacket

....
....
....
....
....

6 in a hospital

....
....
....
....
....

7 in an office

....
....
....
....
....

8 on a car

....
....
....
....
....

32 Choose the answer

Choose the correct answer for each of the following.

1 The words attic, skylight and porch all have something to do with:
   a a theatre   b painting   c a house   d sport
   e cars

2 Which of these is not right?
   a a bunch of bananas   d a dozen eggs
   b a box of matches   e a bar of chocolate
   c a steak of meat

3 If a person is conceited, he or she is:
   a careful   d suspicious
   b shy   e crazy
   c big-headed

4 This is:
   a a safety pin
   b a paperclip
   c a drawing pin
   d a stapler
   e a nail

5 A trunk is part of:
   a a knife   d a telephone
   b a tree   e a television
   c a flower

6 Which of the following would help you see distant objects more clearly?
   a spectacles   d a cheek
   b a telegraph   e binoculars
   c a microscope

7 What is the opposite of rude?

   a certain
   b impolite
   c clean
   d courteous
   e successful

8 Where would you find a sole?

   a on a shoe
   b on a skirt
   c on a shirt
   d on a jacket
   e on a hat

9 To be "broke" is:

   a to be ill
   b to be sad
   c to be without money
   d to be without friends
   e to be in love

10 Which of these words means "hard-working"?

   a flighty
   b industrial
   c job
   d conscience
   e industrious

11 What is this man holding?

   a a dummy
   b a doll
   c a docker
   d a toy
   e a puppet

12 Which of the following is an example of crockery?

   a a knife
   b a car
   c a cup
   d a banana
   e a frying pan

33 The sea-shore

Rearrange the letters to find out the names of the things in the following drawing:

1	R	E	I	L	N		
2	R	O	H	O	N	I	Z
3	E	S	A				
4	H	A	N	D	E	A	L	D
5	Y	U	B	O			
6	V	E	W	A			
7	F	I	C	L	F		
8	V	A	C	E			
9	H	A	B	E	C		
10	C	O	R	K			
11	L	I	G	H	E	N	S
12	B	I	O	L	E	U	Y	F

38

34 Prepositions 2

Fill in the missing prepositions in the following sentences.

1 I'm not very keen .... classical music.
   a of   b on   c for

2 He lives .... the sea.
   a on   b at   c near

3 For the last time – will you listen .... me!
   a to   b on   c at

4 I see that John's finally got engaged .... Janina.
   a with   b by   c to

5 There are too many exceptions .... the rule in English.
   a by   b to   c with

6 My brother's an authority .... women.
   a on   b about   c with

7 Did you receive that letter .... Keith?
   a by   b off   c from

8 His music was inspired .... Beethoven.
   a of   b by   c from

9 Everyone knows that women are equal .... men.
   a with   b among   c to

10 A lot of people were killed .... the war.
   a under   b for   c during

11 You're quite right. I agree .... you completely.
   a with   b on   c by

12 This is something my wife bought me .... my birthday.
   a to   b for   c at

13 Would you like milk or water .... the meal?
   a with   b for   c to

14 I stayed .... a marvellous hotel last summer.
   a on   b by   c at

15 .... you and me, I think our teacher's stupid.
   a with   b between   c among

35 Parts of a car

Match up the following words and numbers:

windscreen wipers . . . . . driving mirrors . . . . . tyre . . . . .

headlight . . . . . bumper . . . . . seatbelt ., . . .

windscreen . . . . . bonnet . . . . . indicator . . . . .

radiator grill . . . . . boot . . . . . number plate . . . . .

exhaust pipe . . . . .

steering wheel . . . . . hand brake . . . . . clutch . . . . .

speedometer . . . . . petrol gauge . . . . . radio . . . . .

foot brake . . . . . accelerator pedal . . . . . horn . . . . .

glove compartment . . . . . gear stick . . . . .

36 Add a letter

Add **one letter** to each of the following words (in any place) to form a new word. A clue is given to help you.

1 RAN	*RAIN*	can spoil a day at the seaside.
2 OAR	....	the sound a lion makes
3 EAR	....	a fruit
4 RULE	....	you use one to draw straight lines
5 COD	....	it is like this in winter
6 MEN	....	the opposite of generous
7 RAM	....	Americans call it a streetcar
8 HAVE	....	something most men do every day
9 SAP	....	keeps you clean
10 EASE	....	artists use one to hold their canvas
11 RAVE	....	it means you are not afraid
12 PEN	....	pubs in England do this twice a day
13 ITCH	....	"supernatural" woman
14 TROLL	....	to walk
15 SORE	....	American word for shop
16 SEAL	....	it is against the law to do this
17 TALE	....	the opposite of fresh (e.g. bread)
18 HARP	....	the opposite of blunt
19 SEE	....	to look for
20 WEAR	....	very tired
21 TIN	....	very small
22 ALE	....	a story
23 LAME	....	seen in a fire
24 FAT	....	people once thought our Earth was this
25 HOSE	....	an animal

41

37 Cartoons

In the following cartoons, the captions (i.e. the words that go with a cartoon) have got mixed up, so that each cartoon has been printed with the wrong caption under it. Work out the correct caption for each cartoon.

Cartoon		Correct caption	Cartoon		Correct caption
1	–	....	6	–	....
2	–	....	7	–	....
3	–	....	8	–	....
4	–	....	9	–	....
5	–	....	10	–	....

1 YOU ARE NOT STILL ANGRY AT ME, ARE YOU, DARLING?

2 DAD, THIS IS TOM, HE WORKS WITH COMPUTERS.

3 SAY CHEESE!

4 BUT WHAT MAKES YOU THINK YOU'VE BEEN WATCHING TOO MUCH TELEVISION, MRS GREY?

5 SORRY, FALSE ALARM.

6 I STILL SAY WE TOOK A WRONG TURNING SOMEWHERE.

7 —MARVELLOUS ACOUSTICS.
—PARDON?

8 ARTHUR'S ALWAYS BEEN A BAD LOSER.

9 RIGHT, WHERE'S THIS SPIDER ON THE CEILING YOU'RE SCREAMING ABOUT?

10 GOT A LIGHT, PLEASE?

38 Too many words

Replace the words in bold type in following sentences with a single word. (The first letter of the world is given.)

1 The reason I like my present flat is that I have such friendly **people living next-door.** (n............................)

2 The "Guinness Book of Records" is published **once every year.** (a....................)

3 After thinking about it for a long time, I finally **made up my mind** to take the job. (d..............................)

4 "I'm frightened", she **said in a very quiet voice.** (w................................)

5 Last week I was **asked if I would like to go** to a birthday party. (i.........................)

6 My **sister's daughter** was taken to hospital last week. (n................................)

7 At the end of the performance, the **people sitting in the theatre** applauded loudly. (a..............................)

8 I was totally **tired and worn out** after the football match on Saturday. (e..............................)

9 A ship could be seen on the **line where the sky seemed to meet the sea.** (h..............................)

10 I can't stand **people who pretend to be good but aren't really.** (h......................)

11 I want you to come here **without any delay whatsoever.** (i................................)

12 I regret to inform you that you have **not managed to pass** the exam. (f..............)

39 British and American English

Fill in the British or American words in the following sentences. Give the British word for sentences 1–5 and the American one for sentences 6–10.

1 Now, madam, if you'd just open the .... , (hood) I'll check your battery for you.

2 It was a black car, Inspector, a Ford I think. But I'm afraid I didn't get a chance to see the .... (license plate)

3 One thing you should remember about England is that people always .... when waiting for (stand in line) a bus.

4 Oh, Peter, I wonder if you could pop down to the .... for me and get a bottle of whisky? (liquor store)

5 I'd like a .... ticket to Hastings, please. (one-way)

6 The baby's crying, darling. I think he wants his .... (dummy)

7 Go and .... before you have a meal, (wash your hands) there's a good boy.

8 There's something wrong with the hot water .... It's running cold. (tap)

9 Excuse me, where's the nearest .... (public con- .... please? venience)

10 We could play a game of poker if someone has a .... of cards. (pack)

Puzzle it out 2 –
Who's who at the party?

Read through the sentences below, then see if you can work out the names of the
people at the party.

Mr Graham has fair hair.

Mr Collins is talking to Mrs Jones.

Mr Jones' wife is not wearing a striped dress.

Father Browne is a priest.

Mrs Collins is talking to Mr Gibson.

The man with Father Brown is married to the woman with dark hair.

Mr Gibson has his back to Mr Graham.

Mrs Collins has long, blonde hair.

The husband of the woman in the striped dress is smoking a pipe.

Number 1 is ....

Number 2 is ....

Number 3 is ....

Number 4 is ....

Number 5 is ....

Number 6 is ....

Number 7 is ....

Number 8 is ....

41 Confusing words

Choose the correct word in each of the following sentences.

1 You haven't (lent/borrowed) my rubber, have you, Paul?

2 He sat down (besides/beside) an old man with a white beard who looked and smelt as though he hadn't washed for weeks.

3 See that large (building/house) over there? Well, that's where I work. I've got an office on the sixth floor.

4 Was it (funny/fun) at the party on Friday?

5 The (nature/countryside) around this town is very flat and uninspiring.

6 The injured man was (laying/lying) on the road close to the wreckage of his car.

7 Who (taught/learnt) you to play the guitar, Fred?

8 Those of you who wish to come to the Zoo this afternoon, please (raise/rise) your hands.

9 When I heard that I'd been given the job I felt very (lucky/happy) indeed.

10 I usually (go up/get up) at 7.30 every morning.

11 Why don't you (take/bring) your girlfriend with you next time? We'd love to meet her.

12 Is it all right if I (go with/follow) you to the concert on Friday, Pam?

13 Sussex is my favourite (landscape/county) in England.

14 I didn't have time to (do/make) the beds this morning.

15 Amsterdam is a city full of (channels/canals).

16 I've been (sparing/saving) for years to buy a house.

17 Would you (check/control) these figures, Mr Brown – just to make sure they're correct?

18 It's a lot of (job/work) looking after children.

19 I prefer to (hire/rent) a television than buy one.

20 The answer to the crossword is on the (backside/back).

21 I thought you said you (were going to/should) give up smoking?

22 Our new neighbours invited me in for a cup of tea this morning. I must say they seem a very (nice/sympathetic) couple.

23 Was it Bell who (invented/discovered) the telephone?

24 I wonder if I might have a (recipe/receipt) for the things I've bought?

25 Oh, Jan, could you (remember/remind) me to phone the dentist this afternoon to make an appointment for Sally?

26 I wonder if you'd mind (bringing/fetching) John from next door? He's wanted on the telephone.

27 What (more/else) did you do in Spain, apart from swimming and sun-bathing?

28 I've just bought a record of Beethoven's Fifth symphony (conducted/directed) by Karajan.

29 When we moved into our new flat I had to sell my (grand/wing) piano because there wasn't enough room for it.

30 We'll have to change the curtains, darling. They don't (pass/match) the new suite. They're the wrong colour altogether.

42 Opposites – verbs

Find the opposites of the words on the left. Choose from the ones on the right. Number 1 has been done for you.

1 to lend	to *borrow*	
2 to vanish	to	
3 to remember	to	
4 to hurry	to	
5 to detest	to	
6 to insult	to	
7 to sell	to	
8 to depart	to	
9 to increase	to	
10 to attack	to	
11 to encourage	to	
12 to expand	to	
13 to improve	to	
14 to punish	to	
15 to support	to	

purchase /buy
decrease
defend
deteriorate /get
        worse
arrive
appear
take one's time
discourage
oppose
reward
forget
borrow
praise
adore
contract

43 Classifications

Write one name for each of the following groups. Before starting, look at the example.

1 Mercury, Mars, Venus, Saturn

2 apricot, date, grape, peach

3 Buddhism, Christianity, Judaism, Islam

4 cathedral, block of flats, museum, department store

5 Swiss, Dutch, Welsh, Belgian

6 golf, polo, rugby, wrestling

7 slowly, better, softly, enthusiastically

8 bow and arrow, dagger, machine gun, hand grenade

9 Gaelic, Hebrew, Yiddish, Swahili

10 leek, Brussels sprouts, turnip, spinach

11 mallet, plane, electric drill, screwdriver

12 pounds, kilos, grammes, ounces

13 corduroy, cotton, satin, crinoline

14 necklace, earrings, locket, bracelet

15 arrowroot, chicory, parsley, sage

16 smallpox, measles, mumps, bronchitis

17 minuet, tango, jive, polka

18 by, from, in, on

19 arson, theft, rape, fraud

20 250, 6, 27, 99

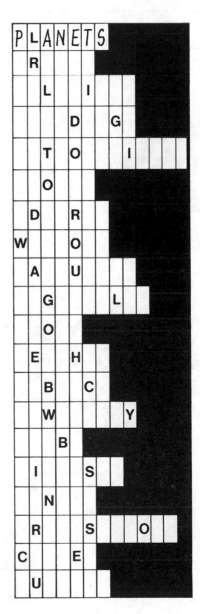

44 Types of transport

Write the number of each drawing next to the correct word or words.

saloon car . . . . .
caravan . . . . .
van . . . . .
hovercraft . . . . .
submarine . . . . .
estate car . . . . .
articulated lorry . . . . .
sports car . . . . .
tanker . . . . .
transporter . . . . .
motorbike . . . . .
yacht . . . . .
coach . . . . .
lorry . . . . .
bus . . . . .
barge . . . . .
ambulance . . . . .
taxi . . . . .
canoe . . . . .
tram . . . . .

45 Synonyms – more adjectives

Give a synonym for each of the words in brackets in the following sentences. Choose from the ones below. Number 1 has been done for you.

giddy	hopeless	immature	amiable
chatty	absurd	reliable	famished
stingy	mad	disgraceful	conscious
intentional	pensive	weird	

1 There's only one way of describing Hitler – he was completely (insane)
   mad

2 A good friend is someone who is kind, considerate and totally (dependable)
   ....

3 Our new boss isn't too bad at all. In fact, she's quite (likeable) ....
   .... really.

4 You are (aware) .... of the fact that he's married, aren't
   you?

5 I wish you'd grow up! You're so (childish) .... !

6 I didn't mean to break it – it wasn't (deliberate) ....

7 That's the last time I go to a party with Simon! His behaviour last night was
   absolutely (disgusting) ....

8 I always get very (dizzy) .... when I stand on the top of
   high buildings.

9 What do you mean you can't afford to buy me a drink? Don't be so (mean)
   ....! You've got a lot more money than I have!

10 I could eat a horse! I'm (really hungry) ....!

11 Take those trousers off – you look (ridiculous) .... in
   them!

12 Our new neighbours are very (talkative) ...., aren't they?

13 You're looking rather (thoughtful) .... this morning,
   Jennifer. What's up?

14 6–1 we lost! 6–1! You played like a team of grannies! You were (pathetic)
   ....!

15 Charles has some really (peculiar) .... ideas sometimes,
   doesn't he?

46 From Bear to Coat

Change the word BEAR into COAT in eleven stages, changing only **one letter** at time.

B	E	A	R
1			
2			
3			
4			
5			
6			
7			
8			
9			
10			
C	O	A	T

1 what deaf people cannot do

2 the noun from hot

3 vegetarians would not eat this

4 e.g. lunch

5 lives in the sea

6 what a salesman must do

7 every church has one

8 something you wear

9 you slide this across to fasten a door or window

10 a young horse

47 Bits and pieces 1

Write the number of each drawing next to the correct word.

hot water bottle	. . . . .
dummy	. . . . .
handbag	. . . . .
hamper	. . . . .
nutcracker	. . . . .
clothes rack	. . . . .
hinge	. . . . .
thimble	. . . . .
curler	. . . . .
razor blade	. . . . .
tweezers	. . . . .
wallet	. . . . .
purse	. . . . .
rawlplug	. . . . .
jackplug	. . . . .

48 Missing words – books, etc.

Put the following words in the correct sentences.

encyclopedia	diary	album
manual	catalogue	register
newspaper	log	calendar
dictionary	cookery book	time-table
directory	map	atlas
index	library	brochure

1 You read a .... to find out what has happened recently, both in your own country and in the rest of the world.

2 A .... is a book or booklet which gives you a list of goods or books for sale, plus their prices.

3 An .... helps you to find the position of a place or a country anywhere in the world.

4 If you can't afford to buy books, then you can always borrow them from the ....

5 An .... is a book (or a set of books) dealing with every branch of knowledge in alphabetical order.

6 You can keep a collection of photographs or autographs in an ....

7 You record personal events and happenings in a ....

8 You look at a .... to know the date and the month.

9 An .... is an alphabetical list at the back of a book of names, subjects, etc. mentioned in it and the pages where they can be found.

10 If you have a .... then you shouldn't get lost.

11 If you want to find out the times of trains or buses you should consult a ....

12 When something goes wrong with your car, you can always try to repair it yourself with the help of a car....................................

13 If you don't know where to go on holiday, why don't you get a holiday ....
.... from your nearest Travel Agency?

14 If you don't know a person's telephone number, you can always look it up in the
telephone ....

15 If you want to find out how to make a particular dish you can look in a ....
....

16 You use a .... to find out the meaning of a word.

17 The captain of a ship fills in a .... every day.

18 You look at a .... if you want to find out how often someone has attended school or a course.

49 Word association 2

Underline two of the words on the right which are associated with or are part of the word on the left. Number 1 has been done for you.

1 BABY   inspire, <u>cot</u>, <u>dummy</u>, creeping, barn

2 DENTIST   meat, toothache, skirt, denture, bore

3 LAW COURT   sentence, dumb, judge, wall, sing

4 SEWING   pattern, stick, tug, stitch, saxophone

5 TRAIN   lucky, compartment, spare, luggage-rack, trap

6 OFFICE   stable, mincer, gem, filing-cabinet, typist

7 PHOTOGRAPH   duck, slides, snapshot, ruler, whisper

8 SEASIDE   bath, stranded, beach, cough, deckchair

9 FUNERAL   coffee, widow, bride, duster, cemetery

10 BIRD   pigeon, trunk, beak, nib, foxglove

11 TENNIS   like, net, offside, umpire, Wembley

12 JACKET   wear, rusty, lapel, smile, crooked

13 RIVER   fly, bank, mining, Danube, cellar

14 NEWSPAPER   circulation, backside, lettuce, editor, reduction

15 BED   headboard, ponytail, slim, blanket, madness

16 CAR   slip, tired, bonnet, deck, radiator

17 CAT   purr, swan, bark, paw, river

18 HOUSE   sob, landing, wind, mortgage, tenor

19 CARDS   joking, clubs, dark, clover, shuffle

20 CHURCH   alter, prayer, hymn, audience, staffroom

50 Bits and pieces 2

Write the number of each drawing next to the correct word.

locket	.....
alarm clock	.....
stamp	.....
kitchen timer	.....
file	.....
egg timer	.....
flippers	.....
pencil	.....
lipstick	.....
compact	.....
cotton reel	.....
headphones	.....
identification disc	.....
decanter	.....
sunglasses	.....

Answers

TEST 1

coat hanger	12
potato peeler	6
lightbulb	2
colander	7
broom	3
plate	4
egg slicer	9
dustpan	8
carpet beater	5
scrubbing brush	10
cheese slicer	11
tea towel	1

TEST 2

1. attractive
2. enjoyable
3. big-headed
4. appalling
5. odd
6. enormous
7. obstinate
8. bashful
9. keen
10. authentic
11. cheeky
12. ample
13. unbelievable
14. vital
15. hilarious

TEST 3

1. house
2. palace
3. monastery
4. convent
5. barracks
6. cell
7. caravan
8. igloo
9. hive
10. nest
11. kennel
12. stable
13. sty
14. web
15. eyrie

TEST 4

Right order:
3 – 8 – 4 – 6 – 1 – 10 – 5 – 9 – 2 – 7

TEST 5

pepper mill	6
liquidizer/blender	12
fire guard	11
bowl	10
tray	7
briefcase	2
lemon squeezer	4
tea strainer	9
bellows	5
bottle opener	3
suitcase	8
ladle	1

TEST 6

1. harmful
2. mean
3. temporary
4. lazy
5. minute
6. hostile
7. exciting
8. timid
9. cheap
10. broad-minded
11. imaginary
12. wonderful
13. sudden
14. uninterested
15. unfortunate

TEST 7

Down
1. Arab
2. India
3. Belgian
4. Czech
5. Canada
6. Swiss
7. Pole
8. Dane
9. Turkey
10. Vietnamese
11. Egypt
12. Swede

Across
1. Finn
2. New Zealand
3. Holland
4. Scotland
5. Australia
6. Greek
7. Jew
8. Peru
9. Norway
10. Eskimo
11. United States

TEST 8

a ball of string
a bunch of grapes
an ear of corn
a cube of sugar
a pack of cards
a crate of beer
a pad of writing paper
a bar of chocolate
a punnet of strawberries
a string of beads
a bouquet of flowers
a quiver of arrows

TEST 9

chopping board	8
aerial	4
banister	11
curtains	1
door handle	12
doorbell	7
coffee filter	5
pillow	10
dustbin	9
umbrella	2
spatula	6
cushion	3

TEST 10

1 (c)
2 (a)
3 (c)
4 (c)
5 (d)
6 (b)
7 (b)
8 (c)
9 (a)
10 (d)
11 (b)
12 (a)

TEST 11

Miss Rees is a cashier
Mr Berry is a caddie
Mr Guard is a caretaker
Miss Knowles is a solicitor
Mr Train is a porter
Mrs Plod is a postwoman
Mrs Carter is a surgeon
Mr Austin is a chauffeur
Mr Field is a farmer
Miss Sayer is a speech thera-
pist

TEST 12

1 ward
2 kitchen
3 cellar
4 attic
5 cabins
6 study
7 crypt
8 hold
9 larder
10 parlour
11 studio
12 lounge
13 dormitory

TEST 13

plane	4
file	6
axe	12
pliers	1
extension cable	5
jack	8
secateurs	9
watering can	10
sickle	3
vice	7
fire extinguisher	11
chisel	2

TEST 14

1 enter
2 vanished
3 purchased
4 detests
5 tripped
6 accomplish
7 altered
8 recollect
9 put off
10 scare
11 spoilt
12 moaning
13 occurred
14 inform
15 bragging

TEST 15

Building number 1 is a church

Building number 2 is an
Estate Agent's

Building number 3 is a museum

Building number 4 is an Art
Gallery

Building number 5 is a bet-
ting shop (Turf accountant's)

Building number 6 is a ci-
nema

Building number 7 is an un-
dertaker's

Building number 8 is an office
block

Building number 9 is the
Town Hall

Building number 10 is a pri-
son

TEST 16

1 car
2 football
3 orchestra
4 flower
5 dog
6 wedding
7 house
8 guitar
9 bed
10 astronomy
11 soldier
12 radio
13 typewriter
14 pub
15 tennis
16 meal
17 river
18 shoe
19 hospital
20 music

TEST 17

stove (cooker)	2
washing machine	4
fridge	10
coffee table	11
bedside table	6
shower	9
bath	3

wardrobe	5	
broom cupboard	8	
fluorescent light	7	
oil lamp	12	
ceiling light	1	

TEST 18

1 big-headed
2 immature
3 intelligent
4 moody
5 sympathetic
6 rude
7 ambitious
8 eccentric
9 obstinate
10 strict

TEST 19

Across
1 orienteering
2 sailing
3 knitting
4 archaeology
5 bridge
6 gardening
7 weaving
8 camping
9 painting
10 table tennis
11 music
12 yoga

Down
1 photography
2 embroidery
3 gliding
4 stamp collecting
5 cycling
6 chess
7 cooking/cookery
8 dancing
9 riding
10 swimming
11 acting
12 ice skating
13 mah-jong
14 billiards

---

15 fishing
16 pottery

TEST 20

1 (b)
2 (a)
3 (c)
4 (b)
5 (c)
6 (a)
7 (c)
8 (c)
9 (a)
10 (b)
11 (b)
12 (b)
13 (c)
14 (c)
15 (a)

TEST 21

shaving socket	7
record storage unit	5
time switch	9
window sill	11
fan heater	1
trolley	2
room divider	12
door knob	8
extractor fan	3
curtain rail	10
coat stand	6
window box	4

TEST 22

Bill is Susan's father
Ted is Susan's brother
Ann is Susan's sister
Freda is Susan's cousin
Olive is Susan's aunt
Paul is Susan's brother-in-law

TEST 23

a pig grunts
a dog barks

---

a mouse squeaks
a cock crows
a frog croaks
an elephant trumpets
a hourse neighs
a lamb bleats
a lion roars
a cow lows

TEST 24

1 throat
2 Saturn
3 wallet
4 rabbit
5 saucer
6 spider
7 willow
8 salmon
9 vanish
10 blouse
11 skiing
12 eighty
13 pigeon
14 lawyer
15 guitar
16 nephew
17 lizard
18 radish
19 petrol
20 gutter

TEST 25

1	rugs	drugs
2	crows	crowds
3	wife	wire
4	daring	darling
5	heard	head
6	bust	but
7	God	Good
8	property	properly
9	polite	police
10	burning	turning

TEST 26

bow tie	9
bowler hat	4
beret	5

cardigan	7
sweater	3
apron	2
gloves	1
braces	10
clogs	6
shorts	11
sandals	12
string vest	8

TEST 27

1	(b)
2	(b)
3	(d)
4	(d)
5	(a)
6	(b)
7	(d)
8	(b)
9	(b)
10	(c)
11	(a)
12	(b)

TEST 28

1	d
2	i
3	g
4	k
5	a
6	j
7	e
8	l
9	b
10	f
11	h
12	c

TEST 29

Order of dialogue part:
- Oh, sorry!
- John! This is a surprise!
- Oh, I live here now.
- Yes, that's right. Sweden.
- About a month ago.
- No, only me.
- Well, as a matter of fact, we've decided to get a divorce.
- Ah well, it can't be helped. And there aren't any children fortunately.
- But anyway, enough of me. What are you doing these days?
- St. Richard's Comprehensive?
- You must enjoy it then.
- (Laughing) I see. Same old John. You haven't changed a bit.

TEST 30

dartboard	6
tennis racquet	3
badminton racquet	8
air pistol	4
golf club	12
tent	2
chess set	11
dice	10
figure skate	13
ski stick	1
shin pad	14
dumbbell	9
shuttlecock	15
binoculars	5
ice hockey stick	7

TEST 31

1 In a school

blackboard
desks
playground
pupils
staffroom

2 In the kitchen

cutlery
dishwasher
fridge
frying pan
sink unit

3 On a boat

crew
deck
funnel
portholes
rails

4 In a church

aisle
altar
congregation
pulpit
pew

5 On a jacket

button
collar
lapel
pocket
sleeve

6 In a hospital

matron
operating theatre
patients
stethoscope
ward

7 In an office

date stamp
filing cabinet
secretary
stapler
typewriter

8 On a car

boot
bumper
clutch
horn
seatbelt

TEST 32

1	(c)
2	(c)
3	(c)
4	(c)

5 (b)
6 (e)
7 (d)
8 (a)
9 (c)
10 (e)
11 (a)
12 (c)

TEST 33

1 liner
2 horizon
3 sea
4 headland
5 buoy
6 wave
7 cliff
8 cave
9 beach
10 rock
11 shingle
12 lifebuoy

TEST 34

1 (b)
2 (c)
3 (a)
4 (c)
5 (b)
6 (a)
7 (c)
8 (b)
9 (c)
10 (c)
11 (a)
12 (b)
13 (a)
14 (c)
15 (b)

TEST 35

windscreen wipers   3
headlight   12
windscreen   4
radiator grill   1
exhaust pipe   9
driving mirrors   5

bumper   8
bonnet   2
boot   7
tyre   10
seatbelt   6
indicator   11
number plate   13
steering wheel   11
speedometer   2
foot brake   8
glove compartment   3
hand brake   6
petrol gauge   1
accelerator pedal   7
gear stick   5
clutch   9
radio   4
horn   10

TEST 36

1   rain
2   roar
3   pear
4   ruler
5   cold
6   mean
7   tram
8   shave
9   soap
10 easel
11 brave
12 open
13 witch
14 stroll
15 store
16 steal
17 stale
18 sharp
19 seek
20 weary
21 tiny
22 tale
23 flame
24 flat
25 horse

TEST 37

1 – 5
2 – 6
3 – 9
4 – 7
5 – 8
6 – 10
7 – 4
8 – 1
9 – 3
10 – 2

TEST 38

1   neighbours
2   annually
3   decided
4   whispered
5   invited
6   niece
7   audience
8   exhausted
9   horizon
10 hypocrites
11 immediately
12 failed

TEST 39

1   bonnet
2   number plate
3   queue
4   off-licence
5   single
6   pacifier
7   wash up
8   faucet
9   restroom
10 deck

TEST 40

Number 1 is Mr Graham
Number 2 is Mr Gibson
Number 3 is Mrs Collins
Number 4 is Mr Jones
Number 5 is Father Browne
Number 6 is Mrs Gibson
Number 7 is Mrs Jones
Number 8 is Mr Collins

TEST 41

1. borrowed
2. beside
3. building
4. fun
5. countryside
6. lying
7. taught
8. raise
9. happy
10. get up
11. bring
12. go with
13. county
14. make
15. canals
16. saving
17. check
18. work
19. rent
20. back
21. were going to
22. nice
23. invented
24. receipt
25. remind
26. fetching
27. else
28. conducted
29. grand
30. match

TEST 42

1. borrow
2. appear
3. forget
4. take one's time
5. adore
6. praise
7. purchase /buy
8. arrive
9. decrease
10. defend
11. discourage
12. contract
13. deteriorate /get worse
14. reward
15. oppose

TEST 43

1. planets
2. fruits
3. religions
4. buildings
5. nationalities
6. sports
7. adverbs
8. weapons
9. languages
10. vegetables
11. tools
12. weights
13. fabrics
14. jewellery
15. herbs
16. diseases
17. dances
18. prepositions
19. crimes
20. numbers

TEST 44

saloon car	12
caravan	5
van	6
hovercraft	7
submarine	18
estate car	19
articulated lorry	1
sports car	10
tanker	11
transporter	13
motorbike	17
yacht	15
coach	20
lorry	16
bus	2
barge	9
ambulance	4
taxi	14
canoe	8
tram	3

TEST 45

1. mad
2. reliable
3. amiable
4. conscious
5. immature
6. intentional
7. disgraceful
8. giddy
9. stingy
10. famished
11. absurd
12. chatty
13. pensive
14. hopeless
15. weird

TEST 46

	bear
1	hear
2	heat
3	meat
4	meal
5	seal
6	sell
7	bell
8	belt
9	bolt
10	colt
	coat

TEST 47

hot water bottle	8
dummy	14
handbag	7
hamper	15
nutcracker	12
clothes rack	3
hinge	11
thimble	2
curler	4
razor blade	10

tweezers   5
wallet   6
purse   13
rawlplug   9
jackplug   1

TEST 48

1 newspaper
2 catalogue
3 atlas
4 library
5 encyclopedia
6 album
7 diary.
8 calendar
9 index
10 map
11 timetable
12 manual
13 brochure
14 directory
15 cookery book
16 dictionary
17 log
18 register

TEST 49

1 cot, dummy
2 toothache, denture
3 sentence, judge
4 pattern, stitch
5 compartment, luggage-rack
6 filing-cabinet, typist
7 slides, snapshot ·
8 beach, deckchair
9 widow, cemetery
10 pigeon, beak
11 net, umpire
12 lapel, wear
13 bank, Danube
14 circulation, editor
15 headboard, blanket
16 bonnet, radiator
17 purr, paw
18 landing, mortgage
19 clubs, shuffle
20 prayer, hymn ("alter" is
   a verb)

TEST 50

locket   11
alarm clock   12
stamp   13
kitchen timer   4
file   9
egg timer   7
flippers   8
pencil   15
lipstick   14
compact   2
cotton reel   5
headphones   6
identification disc 1
decanter   3
sunglasses   10